THE SUBCULTURE
OF VIOLENCE

HASSAN DIBICH

iUniverse, Inc.
New York   Bloomington

The Subculture of Violence

iUniverse books may be ordered through booksellers or by contacting:

iUniverse
1663 Liberty Drive
Bloomington, IN 47403
www.iuniverse.com
1-800-Authors (1-800-288-4677)

ISBN: 978-1-4502-5792-3 (pbk)
ISBN: 978-1-4502-5794-7 (cloth)
ISBN: 978-1-4502-5793-0 (ebk)

Library of Congress Control Number: 2010913486

Printed in the United States of America

iUniverse rev. date: 9/29/10

Acknowledgments

I cannot begin to justify my deepest thanks and sincerest gratitude with the mere embellished monarch of words. To my many friends and relatives who have provided me with steadfast and faithful encouragement and support, *thank you.* I would offer to create a world within which you may partake in this, my life ... through my pen, my truest reality. Because of your care and concern, this is sweetly dedicated to you, dear Concepcion.

In memory of my father, who dedicated his
life in the service of humanity.

About the Author

Hassan Dibich's books include two poetry collections: *Cup of Coffee* and *Warsaw*, and three novels: *The Night of Petersburg*, *The Immortal Tree*, and *Coming to Richmond*. Dibich has lived in Morocco, Belgium, France, England, Costa Rica, and the United States of America.

Table of Contents

List of Figures

List of Tables

Abstract

A number of studies have been conducted around the two theoretically derived models that attempt to explain the subculture of violence thesis. These models are examined from slightly different viewpoints. Homicide has been the traditional violent crime to analyze for either its socioeconomic basis or its inherent cultural effect resulting from growing up in the American South. In addition to homicide, assault and rape are also examined to either support the current thesis or show the inconsistencies in the pre-existing data analysis. The present study examines whether it is the geography of the Southern region or the climate that provokes high crime rates. This study analyzes both the social attachments of children and the type of home that children are raised in for their effects on the crime rates. It is expected that the findings will demonstrate that climate has a stronger relationship to the interpersonal crime rates reviewed, and that in areas where there are many strangers and newcomers, the crime rates are higher. It is also expected that this study will show that children brought up in homes where only a single female parent is present tend to engage in more criminal activity. It is anticipated that the results do not support the tenets of the current thesis proposed by Wolfgang and Ferracuti, which says that a certain segment of the population has a value system that predisposes them to violence. The author suggests that further research in this area be done.

Chapter I: Statement of the Problem

1.1   Summary Description of the Project

There have been a number of studies conducted around the two theoretically derived models that attempt to explain the Southern subculture thesis: (1) the importance of socioeconomic conditions and (2) the existence of a subculture of violence. The traditional violent crime—homicide—has been analyzed for either its socioeconomic basis or its inherent cultural effect that results from growing up in the South. In addition to homicide, assault and rape will also be examined to support the current thesis and show inconsistencies in the previously conducted data analysis. The present study will examine whether it is the culture, geography, or the climate of the Southern region that provokes high crime rates.[1] Both social attachments and the types of home in which children are raised will also be analyzed for their effects on the crime rates. It is expected that the findings of this study will demonstrate that climate has a strong relationship to the interpersonal crime rate; in areas where there are many strangers or newcomers, the crime rates should be higher. It is also hypothesized that children brought up in homes where only a single female parent is present tend to engage in more criminal activity. It is anticipated that the results will not lend the

---

1   This is more fully explained in Chapter III: Methodology.

support to the current thesis proposed by Wolfgang and Ferracuti, which states that a certain segment of the population has a value system that predisposes the violence.

1.2   Introduction

The purpose of this research is to review recent studies and literature on the subculture of violence. This study will then test several hypotheses that may shed light on the subject from a completely different perspective.

Chapter one consists of an introduction, a statement of the problem and its significance, the organization of the study, and the hypothesis that will set the stage for the entire thesis.

Chapter two includes a literature review synthesis that will discuss contributions to the researcher's hypotheses. It also explains the direction of future research and the gaps that exist in the current research on the subculture of violence. The literature review will range from fundamental articles establishing the idea of a subculture of violence to a review of the current literature that relates directly to the hypotheses and methodology, which will be described in the third chapter.

Chapter three integrates the research design, the instruments of research, a description of the unit(s) of analysis, data selection procedures, organization of the data, analyses of the data, how the data will be interpreted, and the findings. The analytical techniques used in this study include correlations, cross-tabulations, and regressions.

Chapter four includes a presentation of the results, as well as the socioeconomic conditions model and the predisposition model.

Chapter five gives a summary, discussion, and several recommendations for the findings from chapter four, appropriately addressing the hypotheses.

1.3   Statement and Significance of the Problem

The thesis of a Southern subculture of violence was most fully developed by Wolfgang and Ferracuti (1967). The essence of their argument is that a certain segment of the population has values that predispose them to violence. The origin of this is believed to be in the socialization patterns particularly unique to the South, in light of slavery and traditional rural surroundings. When violence is perceived as necessary for survival, it is used and thus reinforces the values learned during socialization.

The reason for this thesis is that there are principally two theoretical explanations that have been examined by many researchers trying to find the solution to the higher interpersonal violence rates in the South. However, many questions still exist within their contexts. Additionally, the literature written and published on this controversial topic is conflicting. Some authors agree that there is a predisposition toward violence while others do not.

The significance of this researcher's study is derived from stepping aside from the two traditional viewpoints and from taking a fresh look at the problem, incorporating new variables that may explain this phenomenon more conclusively.

1.3.1   Feasibility and Need for the Study

The need for this study is clear. The conflicting articles written about this topic are not introducing anything new that allows for progress in this field; rather, the authors are rehashing the same variables with different techniques in order to demonstrate that the previous authors' conclusions are invalid.

This researcher's study focuses on new variables that may contribute significantly to the development of a theory in this field. It is possible to use the available data to measure the effects of population shifts, family design, and geographical variables of the South to show new relationships that may affect Southern crime rates.

1.3.2   Definition of Terms

The variables studied and manipulated in this study are the following:

STATE RATES
Homicide 85 – homicides per 100,000 in 1985
Assault 85 – assaults per 100,000 in 1985
Rape 85 – rapes per 100,000 in 1985 (Alaska, 77.2, is treated as missing data)
Murder 60 – homicides per 100,000 in 1960
Assault 60 – assaults per 100,000 in 1960
Rape 60 – rapes per 100,000 in 1960
Population Shift – % population growth (or decline) from 1970-80
Southernness – degrees of latitude south of the North Pole, based on location of state
Warm winter – January average low temperature

The survey information will use the following variables:
SURVEY INFORMATION
Any Arrests – have you ever been picked up by the police?
Year – year of survey
Region – residence in four major regions
Movers – where did you live at age 16? (Region)
Home at 16 – where did you live at age 16? (Family)
Marital Status – current marital status
Divorce – have you ever been divorced?
Parenting – with whom did you live at age 16?
Mom Family – were you raised in a female-headed family?

1.3.3   Limitations of the Study

There are limitations to these data from the standpoint of resources. State rates are used as opposed to SMSAs, which tend to be more accurate. This study only uses one type of regression model, and cites self-reports, in the form of surveys. These impose limitations because other information and analyses may be drawn using different regression models. Self-reporting is not always reliable, especially in the realm of reporting arrests, because of recall bias.

The populations being studied are the following:

Couples – 1980: percent of households that contained a married couple

Male Homes – 1980: homes without an adult female per 1000

Female Headed - 1980: percent of households headed by a woman with kids 18 and under

No Move 60 – 1960: percent living in the same house as they were in 1955

Divorce – 1980: annual number of divorces per 1000 (Nevada 15.4, omitted)

Median Age – 1980: median age of the population

% Poor 79 – 1979: % of families below the official poverty line

% Poor 60 – 1960: % of families below the official poverty line

1.4   Organization of the Study

The researcher will develop arguments and present statistical evidence that will (1) test the current theory adopted by some criminologists that a Southern subculture of violence exists and (2) test whether the high rate of homicides, assaults, and rapes are due to environmental and social factors including temperature, family structure, and level of social attachments. Previous studies will be cited to strengthen the hypotheses and to give supporting documentation of trends noted as early as the mid 1800s.

1.4.1   Conceptual Definitions

There are three conceptual definitions—ideas and hypotheses—that mandate explanation. The first involves physical climate—temperature, as a reason for increased violent crime rates. When temperature increases more people go outside, which allows for more human interaction. Whenever human interaction increases, so does pathological interaction.

The second hypothesis involves social attachment theory. When an individual has social attachments (family, friends, and relatives), the individual is more likely to conform to social norms than someone who does not have these attachments. The idea is to examine people who have uprooted or broken their social attachments through moving around often, or in the case of divorce or death.

The third hypothesis tests the idea that children who grow up in certain types of households will or will not be prone to violent crime. Only traditional homes where a married mother and a father are both present, nuclear families with a parent and stepparent, and households headed by a single parent, will be examined.

1.4.2   Operational Definitions

The effects that will be measured are homicide, assault, and rape for the years 1960 and 1985. These two years are chosen to reduce the chance of an arbitrary increase for one particular year and to measure potential consistency between these violent crimes. The following manipulated effects will be observed: population shifts, Southernness, warm winters, survey information from self-reports on any arrests, year of the survey, residence in the four major regions, location of the individual's home at age sixteen, current marital status, whether or not the individual has ever been divorced, who the individual lived with at age sixteen,[2] in what type of family the individual was raised, the percent of households in the community with a married couple, without a female, and headed by a female, along with the annual incomes to determine the possible effects of poverty on the crime rates.

1.4.3   Summary of Existing Knowledge in the Problem Area

Much worldwide research has been conducted to determine the effects of temperature on crime rates. The tendency has been that in Southern regions where the temperature is high, there is a higher rate of violent crime. In northern regions areas where the temperature is low, there is a higher rate of property crime.

---

2   Age 16 is chosen because that is the minimum age when children may leave home.

Research has also been conducted on the effects of social attachments and the type of family in which one grows up. Current research shows that individuals who grow up in single parent households have an increased chance to engage in violent crime, and individuals without social attachments tend to commit crimes and demonstrate deviant behavior.

1.5   The Hypotheses

Several hypotheses are presented and tested which may bring a new and different perspective to the thesis of a subculture of violence. The hypotheses are:

1) High interpersonal violence rates are higher in the South due to the physical climate rather than a Southern subculture. If the temperature has a positive effect on violent crime, one will expect to see an increase in the violent crime rates in regions where the temperature is high.

2) Social attachments produce conformity. A lack of interpersonal bonds increases violent crime rates. If the number of social attachments increases conformity, then one anticipates a lower crime rate when an individual has many social attachments and a higher crime rate when the individual is socially unattached, as in the case of divorce.

3) Children who grow up in homes without a male presence are more likely to engage in criminal activity, specifically interpersonal crime, than those children who grow up in a traditional nuclear family or a home that resembles one. A family resembling the traditional nuclear family may consist of a parent and a stepparent, or relatives. If children who grow up in the presence of a mother and father (or a model similar to it) tend not to commit violent crime, then children who grow up in single parent families will be more prone to committing violent crimes.

Chapter II: Literature Review

2.1   Literature Review

The idea that a regional culture existed in the South was developed before 1850, but it was never statistically studied in any significant way before 1967. In 1967, Wolfgang and Ferracuti published a book, *The Subculture of Violence.* They focused on the cultural causes of high homicide rates.

Most researchers have focused only on the homicide rates and the effects of subcultural violence (Gastil 1971; Hackney 1969; Messner 1983). Other authors have focused on high homicide rates, stressing the importance of socioeconomic conditions (Blau & Blau 1982; Braithwate 1979; Loftin & Hill 1974; Parker & Smith 1979; Smith & Parker 1980).

Recent studies utilizing models derived from one or both of these theoretical perspectives have provided conflicting results as to the existence, importance, and even the direction of both subcultural and socioeconomic effects on homicide (Bailey 1984; Blau & Blau 1982; Braithwate 1979; Messner 1982, 1983; Parker & Smith 1979; Williams 1984). While the focus on these violence studies has traditionally been on homicide, this researcher will take a different approach and use the data to form more general conclusions that extend to all forms of violent crime, including rape and assault. This study will analyze all three variables in the analyses.

2.1.1 Wolfgang and Ferracuti

Wolfgang and Ferracuti argued: (1) that a certain segment of the population holds values that legitimize the use of violence in some social situations. The origin of such values may be situational; individuals may develop such values because of situational factors via socialization. There may be an interaction between the situation and prior socialization, so that persons whose socialization might predispose them towards the selection of violence may only do so in certain kinds of situations, i.e. those in which violence is perceived as necessary for survival. (2) "That subcultures of violence emerge historically and are characterized by social values that are transmitted during socialization and that govern behavior in a variety of structurally induced situations and may be associated with, but are in no way dependent on, the presence of firearms" (Jo Dixon and Alan J. Lizotte, 1987, p. 385).

2.1.2 Gastil

Gastil believes that the homicide rate is an indicator of the violence that characterizes Southern culture. He begins his studies under the assumption that blacks more often commit murder than whites. He goes on to assume that murder is more frequently committed by those in lower socioeconomic class than those in middle class, by more men than women, and by more Southerners than Northerners. Gastil also states that behavior is patterned in terms of the culture of the actors, a regional culture. Gastil is concerned primarily with the transmission of Southern culture from generation to generation within families and the movements of successive generations among states. He, however, never mentions the possible effects of weather, as in warm winters, or social attachment. Warm weather (either in summer or winter) brings people outside more and, as a result, there is more human interaction. Murder is a crime of interaction, so with warmer weather the amount of interaction, pathological in this case, increases and so does the murder rate. People who have more social attachments conform more than those who don't. When studying migration, this involves broken attachments. The fewer attachments an individual or region typically has, the greater the homicide rate.

Gastil cites previous studies and identifies their strengths and weaknesses in support of his hypothesis. Gastil refers to early studies by Franklin that show the greater tendency for violence in the South as early as pre-Civil War times. This supports the cultural explanation. Neither of these predicts how an individual will behave, but both suggest that past rates in a group are the result of, and result in, a continuing cultural tradition that will tend to produce similar rates in the future, and that external changes in the context of a group will be only slowly reflected in changing behaviors. He mentions that the relative magnitudes of age-standardized murder rates are determined by four additive and interactive conditions or states: (1) the universal conditions of social life; (2) the rates of certain other criminal activities; (3) the extent and severity of a "disorganized condition"; (4) the cultures or subculture of the population.

Gastil's work surrounds the cultures or subculture of the population. It is difficult to define exactly where the influence of Southern culture begins and ends, so Gastil assigns values between five and thirty to show the degree of Southernness in each state. He checks the validity of the regional difference in homicide rates in 1960 and 1980 by using the following variables: percent black, percent nonwhite, size of the white population, percent of the population that is 21-44 years old, percent of the population that is 20-34 years of age, median income, urbanization, city size, median years of education, the number of physicians per 1,000 people, the number of hospital beds per 1,000 people, population size, and the murder to punishment ratio. As the number of hospital beds and physicians increased across the regions, fewer deaths were reported, thus having a reverse effect on the homicide rate. Gastil observed a positive correlation in the lower median income and the number of years of school completed. The lower the population's median income and number of years in school, the higher the murder rate.

Gastil also uses the work of Redfield to expand his theory on the effects of the variables listed previously. It is believed that the homicide rate for blacks in the South was lower than that for whites even though more blacks were killed by whites than vice versa. This is explained by the fact that he collected the data from newspapers, where reporting is not necessarily always accurate.

Gastil reviewed a considerable amount of literature; he references Hoffman's, Brearly's, Porterfield's, Shannon's, and Lottier's statistical data that shows that there is a difference between homicide rates in the North and South. Gastil's work is along the same lines as that done by Wolfgang and Ferracuti. Gastil's historical context is derived from Franklin's work, which he completed as far back as pre-Civil War times. Redfield shows in his work that drunken brawls often led to murder because of the attitude towards and practice of carrying guns and knives. Murders might also occur as a form of revenge for an insult to a person's honor, or simply to show off. Historically, groups attacked other groups out of animosity or for political ends. There were the street duels and night killings, which might have been accomplished by ambush and raids on houses, in which case an entire family may have been wiped out.

When the Southernness factor is removed as a variable and one considers the percent of the population that is nonwhite and those that are between 20–34, there is a negative correlation that indicates that having nonwhites in a state does not contribute to the white homicide rate. Pettigrew and Spier show that the highest positive correlation by states of black homicide rates were also correlated highly with black mobility. Gastil also shows that this may be due to the age factor, 20–34-year-olds, as this particular group is under-reported in the population base, particularly if they are urban blacks.

Redfield believes that black homicide rates were lower than white homicide rates in the South simply because of the poor reporting in the newspapers, which is from where he collected his information. If this is not true, Redfield explains, then it may be due to the fact that blacks were so poor that they could not afford to possess guns or knives. Gibbs found the same relationship that Gastil found among the murder and punishment ratio.

Tittle then makes an even more convincing case for deterrence of murder by severe and certain punishment. Gastil constructs: (1) an

Index of Southernness, which was used in multiple regressions with state homicide rates and was also removed to see the effects of other variables, and whether they were only dependent on the presence of Southernness. Whether Southernness was an independent variable or a dependent variable, it still had a tremendous effect, thus supporting the regional cultural effect. (2) Percent black: Gastil wanted to see the racial effect on the homicide rate. There was a strong positive correlation when used with Southernness. (3) Education: the author wanted to see how the amount of education received by the population affects the homicide rate, as schools were difficult to come by in the South due to the "frontierness." The study found a negative correlation that indicates homicide rates rise as the years spent in school lowers. (4) Income: Gastil wanted to see the effect of income. There was an inverse relationship, which indicates that where the incomes are lower there is a higher homicide rate. (5) Population, age, and urbanity all provided a positive correlation. Medical facilities, including hospital beds, gave an inverse relationship. (6) Murder-punishment ratio: there was a positive correlation, which indicates that certainty and severity of punishment deterred homicide.

Gastil researched what others had found and worked with their statistics to see if their writings and data proved or disproved his hypothesis. Gastil used these writings in his own research to validate his ideas, show their weaknesses, and deliver an alternative viewpoint: his theory. He did the same with the statistics. Gastil selected variables that contributed to the high homicide rate for the South to prove that there is a predisposition to violence. He considers predisposition to violence to be a cultural experience of the region. He looked at the relation of state homicide rates (for whites) to his selected variables and the relation of Southernness Index to see if there were any hidden connections between his variables that might become apparent when the influence of the Southernness aspect was removed. He used the percent nonwhite variable without age and Southernness. It showed that the mere fact of having nonwhites in a population did not increase the homicide rate in and of itself. He found a strong correlation between the number of hospital beds and the number of physicians; they actually decreased the homicide rate because of the medical care that the assaulted victim received.

Gastil collected his data from the World Health Statistics Annual from the World Health Organization. Gastil used the data developed by Brearly for 1920 and 1925, which indicated the number of homicide rates for twenty-four different states to show the historical significance of his research and the regional effect. He also collected figures from 1960 that included a breakdown of the state homicide rates by race: white and nonwhite. The author averaged the homicide rates for 1964-65 and placed them in a figure, spatially arranged. Gastil then assigned a Southernness rating to each of the states, dependent in terms of migration. He did this because the North-South dichotomy was not sufficient at proving his hypothesis. Gastil then collected state homicide rates and proceeded with his statistical analysis by manipulating his variables to substantiate his claim. All of these statistics came from 1960 rates. Gastil's main sources of information came from field research, available data that naturally occurred as he studied the events (not staged), and other data that was not purposely used for studying how homicide affects a region. Gastil used inferential statistics as he was trying to test his hypotheses and to rule out explanations by other scholars in the observed data patterns, relationships, and differences. His analysis techniques were both univariate, where he looked at the effect of one variable, and multivariate as he took more than one variable at a time to see their effects. Gastil first looked at the dispersion among the homicide rates in the United States in order to assign his Southernness indices to the states. He also used a bivariate analysis when looking at the homicide rates among whites and nonwhites. He used the multivariate analysis when testing for spurious correlations. By manipulating different variables Gastil could see the modeling relationships among them and study how each variable, particularly Southernness, affected the other. In the case of the nonwhite population, he used a technique called elaboration.

Gastil did most of his analysis using multiple regressions, which gave him the most information from his data. In preparing the multiple regressions, the author paid close attention to the position of the variables to see if the effect was different in the order of the variables. Gastil was looking to see the effects of this variance. Again, the index of Southernness affected the homicide the most. For example, to test the hypothesis of the murder-punishment ratio, first Gastil had to prepare the data by summing the numbers of imprisonment for homicide and those executed, and then compare those numbers to the murder rates in the states. It was then used as a dependent variable in a multiple regression. The author tried to minimize biases (typically arise from incomplete sampling frames), and incomplete data collection as he used the data collected from the states. Whether this data is already biased is unknown, however, the author gives some explanation to the possible areas of bias. This is namely in the area of the urban blacks as they are a highly mobile group, which could account for the under reporting of the population base. Gastil also relies on census information, which is always biased because a response rate of less than 100 percent represents an incomplete picture. It is even harder to know whether 70 percent responded to the census that year, which is the minimum percentage necessary to produce viable data. Another possible bias could be in the Southernness Index that Gastil formulated based upon his feelings of which states are more Southern than others. Internal validity was observed as the independent variable. Homicide was removed and replaced by Southernness to show that extraneous variables that were removed were not responsible for any unexpected outcomes.

Gastil's research for the most part is objective. The statistics from the states for their homicide records are objective. However, the dependent variables that Gastil chose are objective and slightly biased. He felt that they would somehow have an impact on the homicide rate in order to show perpetuation. As far as the external validity of Gastil's work, it is externally valid because the information is generalizable to the Southern region. He reconfirmed the general assumptions that he began under—that men commit homicide more often than women, blacks more than whites, the lower class more than the middle class, and Southerners more than Northerners.

He also showed that the homicide rate is not necessarily higher in the urban areas. This validates Redfield's hypothesis that increased violence occurs in the South because it is more unsettled and more of a wilderness than the North. Gastil showed a strong correlation between a high homicide rate and the age group 20-34; this group committed more homicides than other age groups. He also showed a relationship between medical attention—measured by the number of physicians, medical facilities, and hospital beds—with the homicide rate. This was an inverse relationship. He confirmed the proposition that education has to do with the homicide rate—that less educated people commit more homicides—which again supports the idea about there being less schools in the other areas, like the East. He also showed his theory that there is a Southernness Index to be considered when looking at the homicide rate.

While the data that he used did prove what he set out to prove, he limited his scope too much. There are other areas that he could have looked into that would have substantiated his hypotheses much more. If he had addressed the weather issue and that of social attachments and perhaps even marital status, his case would be even stronger. What Gastil discovered was that there is a strong correlation between the Southern region and the violence committed there, specifically homicide.

2.1.3 Hackney

Hackney (1969) regressed the 1940 state homicide rates on a variable composed of the eleven confederate states and variables measuring urbanization, education, unemployment, per capita personal income, the state's per capita income, and median age. They ran the analysis separately for blacks and whites in order to control for race.

He claimed that (1) among whites, location in the confederate South was the best predictor of homicide; (2) among blacks, location in the confederate South followed age as the second best predictor. He interpreted these findings that Southerners share a collective perception of violation and persecution, and a cultural tradition that approves of violence as an appropriate response to such perceptions.

He reported that when a regional variable for the South is entered into a regression equation along with a series of socioeconomic and demographic variables, it produces a significant independent effect on the state homicide rate. This effect probably reflects the violent values that are characteristic of the South.

Hackney concludes that Southern violence is a " ... *cultural* pattern that exists separate from current influence" (Hackney, 1969, p. 518).

2.14   Loftin and Hill

Loftin and Hill replicated Gastil and Hackney's studies and added a Gini Index and a Structural Poverty Index to the analysis. The Structural Poverty Index is composed of: (1) infant mortality rates; (2) percent of persons age 25 and older with less than 5 years of education; (3) percent of illiterate population; (4) percent of families with an annual income under $1,000; (5) percent of armed forces who failed a mental test; (6) percent of children living with one parent.

The Structural Poverty Index emerged as the best predictor of the average homicide rate for the years 1959-1961. The indicators of geographically Southern regions were rendered statistically insignificant. The finding confirmed the author's contention that Gastil and Hackney misspecified their models by omitting important variables from their regression equations. They argue that the measurement of the cultural effect by Gastil and Hackney is biased in the direction of the culture of violence hypothesis. Unless it can be assumed that no cultural determinants of homicide correlated with region have been satisfactorily controlled, the regression estimate for the regional variable will represent both cultural and non-cultural effects. Loftin and Hill claim that the only way to assess cultural effects with any degree of confidence is to devise a measure of culture that is independent of region and to enter these measures into the regression analysis.

Loftin and Hill's analysis represents a serious challenge to the subculture of violence thesis. They argue that any effort to infer subcultural effects without the inclusion of direct subcultural measures is inherently hazardous. But to the extent that regional and racial effects can be observed, even with the comprehensive controls for socioeconomic and demographic variables, the subcultural interpretation becomes much more plausible. They find out that a Structural Poverty Index explains how regional and racial compositions affect the homicide rate. Their findings suggest that it was poverty and not region, "Southernness," or racial composition that was related to the variation in state homicide rates.

2.15   Huff-Corzine, Corzine, and Moore

Huff-Corzine et al. replicated Loftin and Hill's research using 1970 state data and a three-year average homicide rate (1969-1971), excluding Hawaii and Alaska from their analysis. They introduce a new measure based on the proportion of the state's population born in the South. In order to gauge the relative influence of poverty and violent cultural values on rates of homicide, they employ a modified version of Loftin and Hill's Structural Poverty Index. They compute separate regression analyses using either Gastil's Southernness Index, or the proportion of the state's population born in the South.

They dealt with multicollinearity by employing a ridged regression. They performed separate analyses using the white homicide rate, nonwhite homicide rate, and the homicide rate for the total population. The results showed that the homicide rate for the total population was significantly influenced by Gastil's Southernness Index, the proportion of the population born in the South, Loftin and Hill's Structural Poverty Index, and percent of the population that is nonwhite. The percent of the population between the ages 20-34, the proportion of the population residing in rural areas, the Gini Index of income inequality, and the availability of hospital beds per 100,000 populations were not significantly related to homicide rate. They found out that Gasti's Southernness Index, the proportion of the population born in the South, and the Structural Poverty Index were significantly related to the white homicide rate. They showed that neither the Structural Poverty Index nor the proportion of the population born in the South were significantly related to the nonwhite homicide rate, although Gastil's Southernness Index was significantly related to the homicide rate among nonwhites. Their findings were contrary to those of Loftin and Hill's 1974 study. They found that violent cultural norms emanating from the South cannot be explained away by socioeconomic inequality or racial characteristics of Southern states but represent an independent source of high rates of homicide.

2.1.6 The Psychological Effects of Weather, Climate, and Seasonality

The assumption that there is an association between weather and human behavior is a tradition dating back some five thousand years ago. Hippocrates attributed the "gentler disposition" of the Asiatics to the temperate nature of their climate (Hippocrates, 1923 [c. 400 B.C.]). In *The Spirit of Laws*, Montesquieu (1955 [1748]) found the people in Southern climates to be "entirely removed from the verge of morality, with passions which are productive of all manner of crimes."

Adolph Quetelet (1968 [1842]) stated that crimes against the person are prevalent in the South and in warmer areas and seasons, while crimes against property are more characteristic of the North and in colder climates and seasons.

Ransom and Morrison, in England and Wales, and Durkheim in France all examined data on crime that called the validity of the apparent association of weather and personal violence into question. Both Morrison and Durkheim argued that rather than climate having a direct effect upon persons that leads them to crime, "the good weather ... multiplies occasions for human intercourse; the multiplication of these facilities arguments the volume of crime; and thus it comes to pass that the conduct of society is, at least, indirectly affected by changes of season and the oscillations of temperature." This established the basic position of the psychological effects of weather and deviant behavior.

Dexter (1904) and Mills (1934) supported the psychological effects of climate, while others continued to challenge any association of weather to homicide.

Schmid's (1904) analysis of Seattle data, Brearley's (1932) analysis of South Carolina homicides, and Cohen's (1941) analysis of early UCR (Uniform Crime Report) data for the United States all failed to find any significant association between climate and deviant behavior.

Pokorny and associates (1963, 1964) reviewed the earlier studies that supported a relationship between weather factors and crime or suicide and found them to be "speculative and ... based on crude data and coarse time intervals" (Pokorny et al., 1963).

An impressive number of state and local studies have tested for a seasonal pattern of homicide and have failed to find such a pattern. Studies have been conducted on this topic by LaRoche and Tillery, 1956 in Tallahassee; Wolfgang, 1958 in Philadelphia; Bensing and Schroeder, 1960 in Cleveland; Deutsch, 1978 in Cleveland; Hisch et al., 1973 in Cleveland; Lundsgaarde, 1977 in Houston; Pokorny and Davis, 1964 in Houston; Munford et al., 1976 in Atlanta; Michael and Zumpe, 1983 in San Francisco, Robertson, 1976 in San Francisco; Deutsch, 1978 in St. Louis, Portland, Los Angeles, Kansas City, Atlanta, Denver, Dallas, and Cincinnati; Block, 1984; Deutsh, 1978 in Boston; Michael and Zumpe, 1983 in Alabama, Arizona, Georgia, Honolulu, Los Angeles, Maine, New Mexico, North and South Carolina, Oregon, Puerto Rico, Tennessee, Texas, and Utah; Lamp, 1983 in West Germany; Block, 1984 in Illinois; Michael and Zumpe, 1983 in Illinois; Blick 1984; Messner and Tardiff, 1985 in Chicago, Canada, California, and New York City; Wilbanks, 1984 in Miami; and Abel et al., 1985 in Erie County, New York. All fail to confirm any significant relationship between climate and violent crime (Cheatwood, 1988).

Yet some major texts still support the belief that violent personal crimes are seasonal (Sutherland and Cressy, 1978). Government reports (Bureau of Justice Statistics, 1983; President's Commission on Law Enforcement and the Administration of Justice, 1967) also support this belief.

Warren et al. (1983) analyzed U.S. mortality data for 1969 through 1978, and Lester (1979) independently analyzed the same data for 1973. Both reached the same conclusions, finding trends in homicide patterns with peaks in July through September (Lester, 1979; Warren et al., 1983).

DeFronzo's 1984 analysis of the 142 largest Standard Metropolitan Statistical Area SMSAs reporting to the UCR found that after nonclamatic variables were controlled for, a "days hot" variable had only a "very weak (and barely significant at the .05 level) association."

Harries and associates (1984) analyzed neighborhoods in Dallas and suggested that social class may be a mediating factor in the effects of heat. That is, "low status neighborhoods showed a more distinct summer peak of assaults than did other neighborhood types."

Baron and Bell (1975) concluded that high ambient temperatures facilitated aggression among subjects who were not already angered, but "actually inhibited such behavior on the part of individuals in the angry condition."

Michael and Zumpe (1983) found that although aggravated assault was significantly related to seasonality in Texas, murder was not.

Block (1984) found that the seasonality in assault figures is in large part a result of seasonal patterns of reporting rather than occurrence. Block has systematically considered the fundamental questions of how one handles seasonality (Block, 1984) and whether crime in general is seasonal (Block, 1984). Her work has discounted a seasonal pattern for homicide in Chicago, Canada, and all other cities and states she examined (Block, 1986; Block et al., 1982). However, she also encountered the paradox discussed. That is, she found some statistical evidence for seasonal variation in homicides in the United States as a whole from 1970 through 1982 (Block, 1984).

Rotton (1986) examined the 1976 homicide rates of forty-one countries and included several climate and sociodemographic variables. He gathered thirty-year average temperatures in January and July in the capital cities of the countries and a variety of other variables such as precipitation, life expectancy, literacy, and kilowatts per capita. The regression analysis yielded equivocal results, with some support for the temperature-aggression hypothesis. But a variety of methodological considerations (e.g. sample size, use of capital cities for assessing temperature distributions, use of thirty-year average temperatures to predict one-year homicide rates) make interpretation difficult. Although the results provide some support for seasonality for homicide, this study is best viewed as too weak to be more than suggestive (Anderson, 1988).

Rotton, Barry, and Kimble (1985) conducted a similar analysis of three violent crimes of homicide, rape, and assault using 1977 crime data from 858 cities in the United States. The results varied somewhat depending on the particular analysis used, but in general, significant temperature effects were observed for all violent crime variables. Once again, this study did not cleanly test the temperature-aggression hypothesis because the climate variables were inappropriate. The study used thirty-year averages and only sampled temperatures in January and July. Thus, the number of hot days in each city during 1977 was estimated only very poorly. The use of thirty-year averages may yield some insight into the long-term effects of climate on the development of subcultures of violence; but they may tell little of the direct effects of temperature within a given year.

Alson collected fourteen social variables for each city, such as unemployment, per capita income, education, age, and racial composition. In the first step of the analysis, social models of crime rate differences among U.S. cities were created for four violent and nonviolent crime indices. The purpose of these models was to partial out the effects of potentially confounding variables. Thus, any variance shared among those predictors and temperature would be assigned to the social variables, not to temperature variables. These models were quite effective; they accounted for 56 percent to 79 percent of crime differences among cities.

In the second step, the study examined climate variables to see if any contributed unique variance in the predication of crime once the social model variables had been entered. As was expected, the various temperature-related variables all contributed significant, unique variance to the predication of violent crime. Temperature did not add anything to the predication of nonviolent crime (Anderson, 1998).

This study provides considerably stronger support for the temperature-aggression hypothesis than previous studies because it avoids many problems present in earlier work. More complete social models of crime were crafted and statistically controlled. Conservative tests of the unique contribution of temperature to crime were used. The tests found that effects of temperature on violent crimes were significantly larger than corresponding effects on nonviolent crimes. Finally, region based temperature effects were assessed at the more precise level of cities (actually SMSAs) rather than a simple/non-south dichotomy.

This researcher will continue the work on developing a positive theory correlating temperature and violent crime rates, using the precedents set by others.

2.1.7   Shaw and McKay

One of the most fundamental sociological approaches to the study of crime and delinquency emanates from the Chicago-school research of Shaw and McKay. As Bursik (1984) and others (e.g. Morris, 1970; Short, 1969) have argued, few works in criminology have had more influence than *Juvenile Delinquency* and *Urban Area* (1942, 1969). In this classic work, Shaw and McKay argued that three structural factors—low economic status, ethnic heterogeneity, and residential mobility—led to the disruption of community social organization, which, in turn, accounted for variations in crime and delinquency (Shaw et al., 1929). However, while past researchers have examined Shaw and McKay's predications concerning community change and extra local influences on delinquency (Bursik, 1987), no one has directly tested their theory of social disorganization (Sampson et al., 1989).

First, most ecological researchers inspired by Shaw and McKay have examined the effects of the characteristics such as median income, racial composition, and residential mobility on crime rates (Kornhauser, 1978; Bursik, 1984; Byrne & Sampson, 1986). While useful as a preliminary test, this strategy does little to verify and refine social disorganization theory since it does not go beyond the steps already taken by Shaw and McKay. As Kornhauser (1978) argues, most delinquency theories begin with socioeconomic status (SES). But the variables that intervene between community structure and delinquency are the issue. To test the theory adequately "it is necessary to establish the relationship to delinquency of the interpretive variables it implies" (Kornhauser, 1978; Sampson et al., 1989).

To be sure, the lack of direct tests of the Shaw and McKay thesis does not stem from a lack of theoretical insight. On the contrary, the major problem has been a lack of relevant data. For example, Reiss (1986) notes that the government gathers very little information on the collective properties of administrative units for which they routinely report information. "Little casual information is available for those same units." Similarly, Heitgerd and Bursik (1987) provide an important test of the ecological implications of social disorganization theory, but conclude that traditional ecological studies (including their own) are not well suited to an examination of the formal and informal networks hypothesized to link community social structure and crime with the same independent variables. Such an examination requires extensive and prohibitively expensive data collection within each of the communities in the analysis (Heitgerd & Bursik, 1987).

Thus, the crux of the problem is that previous macro-level research in crime and delinquency has relied primarily on census data, which rarely provides measures for the variables hypothesized, to mediate the relationship between community structure and crime. Ethnographic research (Suttles, 1968) is an exception to this pattern in that it provides rich, descriptive amounts of community processes central to theoretical concerns. But, as Reiss (1986) argues, ethnographies provide limited tests of theories because they focus on a single community or, at most, on a cluster of neighborhoods in which community properties do not display sufficient variation. While some researchers have examined quantitative dimensions of informal social control (Macoby, Johnson & Church, 1958; Kapsis, 1976; Simcha-Fagan & Schwartz, 1986), their studies have been limited to few select communities, precluding comprehensive multivariate analysis. Consequently, since Shaw and McKay's macro social theory is primarily about *between-community* differences in social disorganization (Kornhauser, 1978), no one has undertaken crucial empirical tests of the community-level implications of the theory (Sampson et al., 1989).

The second reason that Shaw and McKay's theory has not been tested directly is the over-reliance on official crime rates in past research. The general criticisms of official data are well known and extend to official delinquency rates, which reflect ecological biases in official reaction to delinquent behavior (Hagan, Gillis, and Chan, 1978; Smith, 1986; Sampson, 1986). For example, conflict theorists argue that lower-economic status communities may have higher delinquency rates in part because police concentration is greater there compared with high-status areas. Further, communities where police-citizen encounters occur may influence the actions taken by police (Hagan et al., 1978; Sampson, 1986). In support of this idea, Smith (1986) demonstrated that the probability of arrests across communities declines substantially with increasing socioeconomic status—independent of crime type and other correlates of arrest decisions (Sampson et al., 1989).

The reliance on official data leaves open the question of whether Shaw and McKay's findings and the host of census-based studies following them are in part artifactual. In the past twenty years or so, the validity of official statistics has had to rely on self-reported victimization data (Hindelang, Hirschi, and Weis, 1981), but to date, these alternative sources of crime measurement have had little effect on the issue. For their part, self-report studies are typically either national in scope (Elliot & Ageton, 1980), or specific to one locale (Hindelang et al., 1981). Between-community estimates of crime rates based on self-reports are thus nonexistent across a representative number of communities. Victimization rates, on the other hand, have been analyzed across twenty-six cities sampled in the National Crime Survey in the early 1970s (Decker, Shichor, and O'Brien, 1982). But Shaw and McKay's theory is about local community variations in crime rates, not large aggregates such as cities and SMSAs (Bursik, 1984). More importantly, even users of victimization surveys have been forced to rely on census data to measure community structure (Sampson, 1985; Sampson et al., 1989).

2.1.8   Geographic Mobility

Social scientists have long been interested in a potential connection between geographic mobility and various behaviors. One facet of the previous research has focused on the relationship between rates of mobility and crime rates in communities or other social units (Crutchfield, Geerken, and Gove, 1982). The second concerns the effect of individual, geographic mobility on various personal characteristics and behaviors (Rossi, 1980; Rossi & Shlay, 1982; Tittle et al., 1988).

The predominant assumption among social scientists has been that individual mobility, particularly that involving movement from one society or culture to another, leads to deviant or criminal behavior (Cowgill, 1961). Despite contrary views expressed by some (Rossi & Shlay, 1982; Savitz, 1975; Stokels & Shumaker, 1982), numerous theoretical statements have been formulated to explain the generally taken-for-granted association between mobility and crime or other pathological conditions (Angell, 1951; Clinard & Meier, 1975; Friday & Hage, 1976; Glueck & Glueck, 1950; Johnson, 1974; Lauer, 1974; McHugh, 1966; Packard, 1972; Reckless, 1967; Sorokin, 1957; Toffler, 1970). Yet the empirical evidence is weak and contradictory, justifying neither the predominant argument of a mobility effect nor the contrary minority view that no effect exists (Tittle et al., 1988).

Many studies prior to 1960 were interpreted as supporting the assumption of a positive association between mobility and criminal/deviant behavior. However, they were not really capable of demonstrating the effect of residential change on individuals (Cowgill, 1961; Savitz, 1975). Being primarily the ecological type where rates of crime or deviance in geographic areas were correlated with immigration rates or with the proportion of the population that was migrant (Glueck & Glueck, 1950; Robins & O'Neal, 1958; Sullenger, 1950).

Yet, since 1960 at least nine studies, seven of which were able to relate measures of individual mobility directly to individual criminality or deviance, have also reported a positive association between mobility and crime/deviance (Crutchfield, Geerken & Gove, 1982; Shelley, 1980; Buikhuiser & Timmerman, 1970; Kantor, 1965; Green, 1970; Lauer, 1974; Osborn, 1980; Wolfgang, Figlio, & Sellin, 1972; Tittle et al., 1988).

However, at least ten other recent studies, all using individual-level data, have found either association between mobility and deviance (Ball & Bates, 1966; Barrett & Noble, 1973; Butler, McAllister & Kaiser, 1973; Cowgill, 1961; Hunt & Butler, 1972; Simpson and Van Arsdol, 1967), a negative rather than a positive association (Savitz, 1975), or mixed results for different categories of migrants (Kinman & Lee, 1966). Furthermore, some researchers have observed that documented positive associations are probably spuriously attributable to other variables (Crutchfield, Geerken & Gove, 1982; Jensen & Rojek, 1980; Kantor, 1965; Sullenger, 1950). Evidence in two studies points to the possibility that associations between mobility and crime/deviance may reflect the effects of crime on mobility rather than the reverse, as is usually assumed (Osborn, 1980; Robins & O'Neal, 1958; Tittle, 1988).

In short, the evidence concerning effects of geographic mobility on criminal or deviant propensities of individuals is contradictory. Even if all the current evidence were in agreement, little would still be known about the effects of mobility on the probability of deviant or criminal behavior. This is because: (1) typically, measures of crime or deviance have been drawn from official records of control agencies, raising the possibility that the findings are biased by expectations among control agents; (2) most studies do not control for variables that might render an association between migration and deviance that is spurious or that might suppress an actual relationship; (3) investigators have rarely considered variations in frequency, recency, or distance of moves, the usual practice being to dichotomize cases as migrant or nonmigrant (Lauer & Lauer, 1976); (4) the actual processes by which mobility and crime/deviance might be interlinked have scarcely been studied empirically; (5) no systematic comparisons have been made of the effects of mobility on different kinds of crime/deviance; (6) no studies have explicitly estimated the possible reciprocal effects of crime/deviance and mobility. Researchers in almost all cases have assumed that mobility must influence deviance but do not allow for deviance to influence the likelihood of mobility (Tittle et al., 1988).

This study will focus on the correlation between data gathered from state arrest rates and self-reported arrest surveys regarding where the individual lived at age sixteen and other factors that contribute to mobility, such as divorce.

Chapter III: Methodology

3.1 The Research Design

The effects that will be measured are homicide, assault, and rape for the years 1960 and 1985. These two time frames are chosen to reduce the chance of an arbitrary increase for one particular year and to measure potential consistency or recurring trends. The data comes from state rates as tabulated in the UCR (Uniform Crime Report), which is contained in the diskette designed by Rodney Stark. The manipulated effects will be observed using population shifts, Southernness, warm winters, survey information, the General Social Survey form on arrests, year of survey, residence in the four major regions, location of the individual's home at age sixteen, current marital status, whether or not the individual has ever been divorced, with whom the individual lived at age sixteen, in what type of family the individual was raised, the percent of households with a married couple, without a female, and headed by a female along with the annual incomes to determine the possible effects of poverty on the crime rates.

3.1.1 Data Collection Produce

This study uses data contained on the diskette *Showcase Live by Rodney Stark*. There are two major components of this software.

"States" in the aggregate database, consists of seventy-three variables from the fifty states and includes recent official crime statistics from the *Uniform Crime Report,* published annually by the Federal Bureau of Investigation. "Survey" is the individual-level database. It consists of thirty-eight variables for 2,977 respondents from the 1973 and 1984 General Social Surveys—national samples of Americans who are eighteen and over. This database, a national probability sample, includes self-report items on arrest and crime victimization. For example, it contains questions such as: Did you ever receive a traffic ticket; Were you ever charged by the police; Have you ever been threatened with a gun or shot at; and Have you ever been punched or beaten by another person?

3.1.2   Observations and Measurement

Because the data is already contained on the diskette, the observations and measurements reflect the manipulation of the data that already exists on the diskette. The data on the diskette was correlated, cross-tabulated, and also used in regression analysis.

The advantages of using this type of information are that the information is already collected, which saves time and money, and the program includes statistical procedures that may be easily manipulated. The disadvantages of using this type of database are that there could be errors in the transcription of information to the diskette, which would be perpetuated unknowingly, and the data collection is limited to the time periods selected by the creator.

3.2   The Instrument

After using the tutorial and workbook in order to learn how to use the program, the validity was tested using several examples such as, "Do states with higher church membership rates have lower crime rates?" Other questions include: "What kinds of people, and in what areas, are afraid to walk in their neighborhoods at night?" And, "What factors influence support for capital punishment?" The reliability of the program rests in the actual validity and reliability in the original gathering of the data by the individuals who compile the UCR. The data on the diskette will be only as reliable and valid as the data contained in the UCR. Because all the information is contained on the diskette, there is no applicability of (1) scoring and coding and (2) procedures for administering the questionnaire or collecting data.

The survey instrument was the UCR, which has been used since 1929 to gather national statistics about arrests.

3.3   Description of subjects or other units of Analysis

The purpose of the research is to determine the effects of climate, social attachments, and the family circumstances of interpersonal violence rates. The units of analysis are numerous. The dependent variables are the arrest rates for homicide, assault, and rape. The independent variables are (1) mobility rate, (2) national population shift, and (3) personal information including: age, marital status, income, arrest history, and family unit type. Specifically, the independent variables are:

STATE RATES – from *Showcase Live*
   Homicide 85 – homicides per 100,000 in 1985
   Assault 85 – assaults per 100,000 in 1985
   Rape 85 – rapes per 100,000 in 1985 (Alaska, 77.2, is treated as missing data)
   Murder 60 – homicides per 100,000 in 1960
   Assault 60 – assaults per 100,000 in 1960
   Rape 60 – rapes per 100,000 in 1960
   Population shift – percent of population growth (or decline), 1970-80
   Couples – percent of households that contained a married couple in 1980
   Male homes – homes without an adult female per 1,000 in 1980
   Female Headed – percent of households headed by a woman with kids 18 and under in 1980
   Divorce – annual number of divorces per 1,000 in 1980 (Nevada,15.4, is omitted)

Median Age – 1980: median age of the population

Southerners – degrees of latitude south of the North Pole, based on location of state

Warm winter – January average low temperature

No Move 60 – percent living in same house in 1960 as in 1955

% Poor 79 – percent of families below the official poverty line in 1979

% Poor 60 – percent of families below the official poverty line in 1960

SURVEY INFORMATION – from *Showcase Live*

Any Arrests – have you ever been picked up by the police?

Year – year of survey

Region – residence in four major regions

Movers – where did you live at age 16? (Region)

Home at 16 – where did you live at age 16? (Family)

Marital Status – current marital status

Divorce – have you ever been divorced?

Parenting – with whom did you live with at age 16?

Mom family – were you raised in a female-headed family?

3.4   Sampling Procedure or Other Data Selection Procedures

Rodney Stark did the original sampling procedures and data selection. In terms of the General Social Survey, the 1973 data was collected using the modified probability sample, and the 1984 data was collected using a full probability sample. The subjects sampled were chosen from either Standard Metropolitan Statistical Areas or from non-metropolitan counties that were selected in National Opinion Research Center's Master Sample. These are in accordance with the method of probabilities proportional to size.

The major differences between a modified probability sample versus a full probability sample are differences in the sample number—individuals as opposed to residential sampling.

3.5   Analysis of the Data

The data will be analyzed using the variables and statistical procedures that are available in the software *Showcase Live*. This study used state rates when examining the first hypothesis, which is concerned with physical climate and interpersonal violence. Survey information was used in the second and third hypotheses, which studied the relationship between social attachment theory and interpersonal violence, and the relationship between family structure and interpersonal violence, respectively.

3.6   How the Data Will be Interpreted

The .05 and .01 significance levels will be used to determine the levels of significance of the correlations. A significance level of .01 indicates that there is a 1 in 100 chance of the data being randomly correlated.

Regression analysis was also used to assess the variance in the dependent variables attributable to the independent variables.

3.7   Findings

The findings will be communicated using tables and figures of actual correlation, cross-tabulation, and regression analyses. These will be accompanied by a description of the particular table or figure. For example, the first of two theoretically derived models emphasizes the importance of socioeconomic conditions. In other words, there is a relationship between poverty and state homicide rates (Loftin & Hill, 1974; Messner, 1983). It is postulated that there is a link because of the frustrations that result when a person is not able to cope with the everyday economic problems. This may cause one to lash out violently. Figure 1 shows the correlation between percent poor 79 (1979, percent of families below the official poverty line), homicide 85, assault 85, and rape 85 (1985, the number of rapes per 100,000 people).

Figure 1

Correlations Between Percent Poor 79 and
Homicide 85, Assault 85, and Rape 85

Homicide 85	Assault 85	Rape 85
** 0.49	0.18	0.05
(50)	(50)	(49)

Significance levels: * .05, ** .01

There is a positive correlation between percent poor 79 and the homicide rate; but, there is almost no correlation between percent poor 79 and assault 85, or between percent poor 79 and percent rape 85.

Figure 2

Correlations Between Percent Poor 60 and
Murder 60, Assault 60, and Rape 60

Murder 60	Assault 60	Rape 60
*** 0.60	* 0.32	-0.11
(50)	(50)	(50)

Significance Levels: *.05, **.01

Nearly the same data exists from 1960 rates. See figure 2 above. There is a strong relationship between percent poor 60 and murder 60 and a weaker relationship between percent poor 60 and assault 60.

Chapter IV: Presentation of Results

4.1   Socioeconomic Condition and Violence

The first of two theoretically derived models emphasizes the importance of socioeconomic conditions. In other words, there is a relationship between poverty and state homicide rates (Loftin & Hill, 1974; Messner, 1983). This relationship may exist because of the frustrations that result when a person is not able to cope with the everyday economic problems and violently lashes out as a result. Figure 1 shows the correlation between percent poor 79 (1979, percent of families below the official poverty line) and homicide 85, assault 85, rape 85 (1985, per 100,000 people).

Figure 1

Correlations between Percent Poor 79 and Homicide 85, Assault 85, and Rape 85

Homicide 85	Assault 85	Rape 85
** 0.49	0.18	0.05
(50)	(50)	(49)

Significance Levels: * .05, ** .01

There is a positive correlation between percent poor 79 and the homicide rate but almost no correlation between percent poor 79 and assault 85, and between percent poor 79 and rape 85.

Figure 2

Correlations between Percent Poor 60 and Murder 60, Assault 60 and Rape 60

Murder 60	Assault 60	Rape 60
** 0.60	* 0.32	-0.11
(50)	(50)	(50)

Significance Levels: * .05, ** .01

Nearly the same data exists from 1960 rates. See figure 2 above. There is a strong relationship between percent poor 60 and murder 60 and a weaker relationship between percent poor 60 and rape 60.

Figure 3

Regression using Percent Poor 79 and Southernism as the Independent variables and Homicide 85, Assault 85, and Rape 85, as the Dependent Variables

	Homicide 85	Assault 85	Rape 85
% Poor 79 Beta	0.13	-0.15	-0.20
R*	0.51	0.19	0.05
Southern Beta	0.65	0.59	0.41
R	0.73	0.50	0.30
Explained Variance	54%	26%	11%

*Correlation value
Significance Level: 0.05

Figure 4

Regression Using Percent Poor 60 and Southernism as the Independent Variables and Murder 60, Assault 60, and Rape 60 as the Dependent Variables

	Murder 60	Assault 60	Rape 60
% Poor 60 Beta	0.21	-0.15	-0.45
R	0.64	0.30	-0.09
Southernism Beta	0.71	0.74	0.59
R	0.84	0.66	0.32
Explained Variance	73%	44%	23%

Significance Level 0.05

In addition, if one takes a look at the regression between percent poor 79, Southernism (indicating the Southern United States), and the homicide rate in figure 3, it also confirms that socioeconomic class does not have a significant effect on the homicide rate. The correlation value is 0.51 but the beta weight is only 0.13; whereas with Southernism, the "R" value is 0.73 and the beta weight is 0.65. The results indicate that the homicide rate has a greater relationship with region than poverty. The same concept also applies to assault 85 and rape 85, which are also shown in the regression in figure 3. A regression was also run for the 1960 rates to further document that poverty does not account for much of the variance. See figure 4.

4.2   Predisposition Model

The second of two theoretically derived models postulates the existence of a group predisposed to violence via their upbringing; violent behavior is instilled by virtue of being born and raised in the South. This premise is in and of itself false because being born and raised in the South, a region, does not have an effect on the homicide rate. To suggest that it has an effect on the homicide rate would be erroneous. The question then arises: is it a particular way that children are brought up that makes their behavior more violent? It is important to look first at how the South is populated in relation to other regions of the country, and then look at how the South is populated within its own region.

Figure 5

Cross-tabulation Between Region and Movers, 1973

Category: 1973
Control: Year
Row: Region
Column: Movers[3]

	Here	Different City	Different State	Total
East	21.6%	24.6%	22.6%	22.7%
South	36.5%	27.8%	29.4%	31.9%
West	11.5%	18.4%	22.5%	17.0%
Midwest	30.4%	29.2%	25.5%	28.4%
Total	100%	100%	100%	100%

---

3   See Appendix B for definition

Figure 6

Cross-tabulation Between Region and Movers, 1984

Category: 1984
Control: Year
Row: Region
Column: Movers

	Here	Different City	Different State	Total
East	22.6%	17.9%	18.7%	20.0%
Midwest	32.3%	35.3%	17.6%	28.3%
South	35.0%	30.7%	34.0%	33.5%
West	10.1%	16.1%	29.7%	18.2%
Total	100%	100%	100%	100%

A cross tabulation was constructed using regions and the proportion of its residents still living where they were born, those who have moved to another city, and those who have moved to another state. This was shown for two separate years, 1973 and 1984, to show any fluctuations in the population that might have an effect on the interpersonal violence rates. Figures 5 and 6 above are the respective cross tabulations.

The South was the most populated region of the country for both years in question. The South is even more populated in the 1984 data than the 1973 data by 1.6 percent. This is a rather significant finding, which may account for the higher proportion of violence through mere population numbers. It should also be noted that more Southerners remain in the place where they were born; whereas, people from the Midwest tend to move to other cities and Easterners and Westerners move to other states. The total populations of the Midwest in both sets of data have remained virtually the same. The total populations of the East have decreased significantly, by almost 3 percent. The population in the West has increased a little over 1 percent. Could it be true that the populations in the South and West are increasing due to the influx of people from the East?

With the population remaining stable for those born and raised in the South, is the rate of violence increasing because more people are committing violent acts more often than once? Could the increase in violence possibly be attributable to the increase in population, due to those moving into the South from other regions? In this case, there is no such cultural predisposition for Southerners; the rates are being examined for the violence committed by the others moving into this region. If it is true that Southerners are committing multiple acts of violence, then the thesis needs more scrutiny by utilizing other variables. This is an area for further study.

Figures 7, 8, 9, 10, and 11 indicate distributions of the population within the Southern region. These distributions are divided into the following areas: rural, town, medium-sized city, suburb, and big city. Again, the regions and location of where the population was born are the variables. Historically, Southerners have lived in rural areas.

Figure 7

Cross-tabulation Between Region and Movers Using Home at 16 as the Control and Rural as the Category 9

Control: Home at 16
Category: Rural
Row: Region
Column: Movers

	Here	Different City	Different State	Total
East	11.1%	8.8%	17.6%	12.7%
Midwest	29.8%	35.5%	24.7%	29.6%
South	51.4%	41.8%	34.9%	43.3%
West	7.7%	13.9%	22.8%	14.4%
Total	100%	100%	100%	100%

The data shows that most Southerners continue to live in rural areas, more than in any other region (East, Midwest, and West). In fact, Southerners are most likely to live in smaller communities in general as established by the data.

Figure 8

Cross-tabulation between Region and Movers Using Home at 16 as the Control and Town as the Category

Control: Home at 16
Category: Town
Row: Region
Column: Movers

	Here	Different City	Different State	Total
East	21.7%	22.7%	17.9%	20.6%
Midwest	28.6%	29.8%	22.6%	26.8%
South	38.3%	31.8%	30.6%	33.8%
West	11.4%	15.7%	28.9%	18.8%
Total	100%	100%	100%	100%

Figure 9

Cross-tabulation between Region and Movers Using Home at 16 as the Control and Medium City as the Category

Control: Home at 16
Category: Med. City
Row: Region
Column: Movers

	Here	Different City	Different State	Total
East	25.2%	30.3%	19.2%	27.7%
Midwest	30.0%	27.0%	19.8%	25.8%
South	27.0%	14.6%	29.8%	25.1%
West	17.8%	28.1%	21.4%	21.4%
Total	100%	100%	100%	100%

Figure 10

Cross-tabulation between Region and Movers Using Home at 16 as the Control and Suburb as the Category

Control: Home at 16
Category: Suburb
Row: Region
Column: Movers

	Here	Different City	Different State	Total
East	33.7%	30.8%	19.2%	28.2%
Midwest	30.1%	25.6%	19.2%	25.2%
South	25.3%	17.9%	35.6%	26.1%
West	10.9%	25.7%	26.0%	20.5%
Total	100%	100%	100%	100%

Figure 11

Cross-tabulation between Region and Movers Using Home at 16 as the Control and Big City as the Category

Control: Home at 16
Category: Big city
Row: Region
Column: Movers

	Here	Different City	Different State	Total
East	34.4%	34.0%	28.0%	32.3%
Midwest	39.9%	42.4%	16.1%	32.7%
South	15.6%	11.8%	26.5%	18.4%
West	10.1%	11.8%	29.4%	16.6%
Total	100%	100%	100%	100%

It has been suggested by other researchers that Southerners live in more rural areas than urban areas; if this is true and there is a Southern subculture of violence, then one would expect to see a higher proportion of crimes reported in the rural areas. To test this, a cross tabulation was constructed using region, urban/rural areas, and arrests.

Figure 12

Cross-tabulation between region and Urban/Rural Using any Arrests as the Control

Control: Any arrests
Category: Yes
Row: Region
Column: Urban/Rural

	Big City	Suburb	Town	Rural	Total
East	23.2%	17.7%	16.5%	6.7%	17.58%
Midwest	27.3%	27.1%	28.1%	26.6%	27.6%
South	23.2%	21.9%	31.4%	40.0%	27.9%
West	26.3%	33.3%	24.0%	26.7%	26.7%
Total	100%	100%	100%	100%	100%

Figure 12 shows the results from the tabulation of data. Indeed there is a greater proportion of arrests reported in rural areas of the South; but, when comparing the totals for all of the regions, there is no difference in the arrest rates except for the east, at 17.8 percent. The South, West, and Midwest are 27.9 percent, 26.7 percent, and 27.6 percent respectively. Does this imply that fewer people are arrested in the east for their crimes; or does it imply that more people are arrested for their crimes in other regions? Is there a difference in the criminal justice systems of each region; or could it be that there is no subculture of violence based on crime rates—that it is influenced by some other entity? Could it possibly be that the people who are arrested are arrested for more violent crimes than other types of crime? It is impossible to answer all of these questions from the data provided. If there were categories of the arrests, more information could be derived. Again this is another area that needs more conclusive studies to be conducted.

Chapter V: Summary, Discussion, and Recommendations

5.1   Climate and Culture?

Monthly crime rates fluctuate, depending on the season. Crime rates tend to be higher in the summer months than in the winter months. Specifically, homicide, assault, and rape occur much more frequently in the summer than in the winter. See table 1 below.

Table 1

Cross-tabulation Between the Distribution of Violent Crime and the Following Months

Violent Crime	January	February	July	August
Homicide	7.7%	7.0%	9.4%	9.4%
Assault	6.8%	6.3%	10%	10%
Rape	7.1%	6.7%	9.8%	10.2%

These rates are national rates from the UCR (Index of Crime, 1986-90), which demonstrate the seasonality of violent crimes. However, if one looks at the rates in places with warm winters, like the South, the regional rate accounts for more than forty percent of the total national annual rate. This is where the definition of interpersonal violence requires contact between two or more people. Warm weather brings out more human interaction which then creates more opportunity for the possibility of violence. The correlations below substantiate this claim.

Table 2

Correlations between Warm Winters and Homicide 85, Assault 85, and Rape 85[4]

Homicide 85	Assault 85	Rape 85
**0.61	**0.48	**0.52
(50)	(50)	(49)

Significance Levels: * .05, ** .01

---

4   See Appendix A for definition

Table 3.1

Regression using Warm Winters and Southernness as the Independent Variables and Homicide 85, Assault 85, and Rape 85 as the Dependent Variables

	Homicide 85	Assault 85	Rape 85
Warm Winters Beta	0.50@	0.70	0.87
R	0.77+	0.68+	0.60+
Southernness Beta	0.35@	-0.03	-0.36
R	0.73+	0.50	0.30
Explained Variance	64%	46%	42%

+ indicates significant finding @[5]

---

[5]   Due to the high Intercorrelation between Warms Winters and Southernness, there is a problem of multicollinearity between these variables and this finding should be interpreted with caution. See Table 4.

Table 3.2

Regression using Warm Winters and Southernness as the Independent Variables and Homicide 60, Assault 60, and Rape 60 as the Dependent Variables

	Homicide 85	Assault 85	Rape 85
Warm Winters Beta	0.20@	0.42	0.53
R	0.72+	0.67+	0.47+
Southernness Beta	0.68@	0.34	-0.07
R	0.64+	0.66+	0.32
Explained Variance	72%	51%	22%

+ indicates significant finding
@ See footnote 14

The regression in tables 3.1 and 3.2 also shows the strong relationship between warm winters and homicide/assault/rape for both 1985 and 1960. The variables show a strong relationship between Southernness and homicide 85 and 60 and assault 60; however, there are significant relationships between all variables and warm winters. To base an entire thesis on the positive regression for Southernness when there is a more significant finding using warm winters shows that the tenets of the subculture of violence thesis cannot all be explained, as past researchers would like to entertain.

Based on the data, the findings indicate the Southern region's higher crime rate is not indicative of the subculture of violence; rather it is due to the physical climate of the region. The more people have the opportunity to interact, the more possibility exists for pathological interaction.

Table 4

Correlations of Homicide 85[6]

If homicide is replaced with assault and rape, the following correlations are made. Note that the remainder of the correlations, i.e. two through nine, remains the same as it appears in table 4 and so it is not shown again.

	1	2	3	4	5	6	7	8
Homicide 85	1.00							
Population Shift	*.29	1.00						
Couples	**-0.37	0.07	1.00					
Male Homes	0.06	**0.46	**-0.55	1.00				
Female Headed	**0.57	-0.19	**-0.52	-0.16	1.00			
Divorce	**0.41	**0.67	0.21	0.22	-0.12	1.00		
Median Age	-0.16	*-0.32	*-0.29	0.03	-0.13	-0.20	1.00	
Southernness	**0.73	0.23	0.01	**-0.36	*0.29	*0.31	-0.07	1.00
Warm Winters	**0.61	**0.39	-0.22	-0.05	**0.33	*0.32	0.0	**0.75

---

6   See Appendix A for definition.

Table 5

Correlates of Assault 85 and Rape 85

	1	2	3	4	5	6	7	8
Assault 85	*.29	**-.47	.19	**.56	*.26	-.07	**.50	**.48
Rape	**.39	**.48	**.38	**.50	*.33	-.08	*.30	**.52

Significance Level: 0.01

Table 4 shows the correlations for several variables with homicide 85. Table 5 shows the correlations for those same variables with assault 85 and rape 85. These tables reveal several interesting relationships. First, the correlation shows that children raised in a male-headed household are less likely to commit homicide. Male-run homes are also more likely to move around, perhaps due to job-related moves.

The divorce rate strongly correlates with the shift in population (0.67). Population shifts correlate strongly with warm winters (.39). Female-headed households tend to be in warm winter regions as well, as shown by the strong correlation between them (.33). Of course, one would expect warm winters and Southernness to correlate highly because of the geographical location of the South.

From examining table 5, again male-headed homes (without a female present) correlate poorly with assault, but male-headed homes correlate strongly with rape. This could potentially be another area of further research to determine why this relationship exists. This study uses median age as the variable to see if multicollinearity is a significant problem. When the data is tested, it does not seem to be a problem. However, there is a problem with multicollinearity between Southernness and warm winters. In addition, the homicide, assault, and rape rates are from 1985, not an average of three or more years as is desired to rule out any abnormal fluctuations in the crime rate for the particular year.

5.2 Social Attachment and Interpersonal Violence

The second stated hypothesis of this study has to do with social attachments and conformity or nonconformity to the law, and how this affects interpersonal crime rates. By examining the correlations in table 4 and 5, the variables that are meaningful in the discussion of social attachments are (1) population shift, because when one moves, bonds are broken and new ones have to be developed. This takes time when one is in a new area. (2) Divorce, because it implies moving, which is valid according to the co-relational data; and (3) couples, because they are the foundation of social attachments for the unit itself and for the family those bonds create.

Noting the correlation between couples and population shift (.07), one may conclude accurately that couples do not move very much since the value is nearly zero; whereas, the incidence of divorce correlates quite significantly with population shift.

The rationale for choosing this is that many crime theories comment on the necessity of social attachments and interpersonal relationships in maintaining conformity. The reason for this is that conformity is an integral part of preserving those relationships with others. Theories of social integration demonstrate that crime rates are lower in areas with a population that has strong bonds within it. Therefore, one would expect that areas with a large number of couples, a low divorce rate, and a small population shift would have a low crime rate. This will be analyzed at the state level and the individual level through surveys.

Once again returning to tables 4 and 5, there is no relationship between Southernness and population shift, but there is a significant relationship between warm winters and population shift.

Table 6

Regression using Population Shift, Couples, and Divorce as Independent Variables and Homicide 85, Assault 85, Rape 85, Warm Winters and Southernness as Dependent Variables

	Homicide 85	Assault 85	Rape 85	Warm Winter	Southernness
Pop. Shift Beta	0.03	0.33	0.25	0.41	0.11
R	0.24	0.29	0.29	0.39	0.26
Couples Beta	-.45	-.60	-.57	-.34	-.07
R	-.34	-.47	-.43	-.21	0.02
Divorce Beta	0.48	0.16	0.30	0.11	0.25
R	0.41	0.26	0.33	0.32	0.31
Explained Variance	35%	42%	42%	26%	11%

Significance level: 0.01

The multivariate regression in table 6 shows the rates of the effects of population shift, couples, and divorce on homicide 85, assault 85, and rape 85. A regression has also been done to see how warm winters and Southernness affects each of these. Examining each category, one can deduce that population shift does not have a meaningful relationship to homicide, but it does appear to affect assault and rape. Couples influence homicide 85, assault 85, and rape

85 significantly in an inverse relationship rather than a direct one, which is what this researcher had anticipated.

In the table, divorce shows a strong relationship to homicide, but not assault. It shows a weaker relationship to rape. The conclusion drawn from this is that these indicators of interpersonal bonding do affect the crime rate in a significant way, which supports the hypothesis.

Looking at this data from the perspective of regional effects, one would think to ask: are these variables affected more by region or by climate? The answer is by climate. Population shifts seem to occur more often in warm winter climates, again verifying the hypothesis. Divorce, however, has no meaningful relationship to climate but more to region. Each of these increases the crime rates. Tables 3.1 and 3.2 show that warm winters account for most of the influence that Southernness may have shown in correlations.

Table 7

Cross-tabulation Between Any Arrests and Marital Status

Row: any arrests
Column: marital status

	Married	Single	Divorced or Seperated	Widowed	Total
No	89.9%	82.1%	81.0%	95.1%	88.2%
Yes	10.1%	17.9%	19.0%	4.9%	11.8%
Total	100%	100%	100%	100%	100%

Table 7 above shows the data collected from surveys on marital status and any arrests. There are limitations to the amount one can infer from this data, as it is not known what these arrests are for; but the data does substantiate that the lack of social attachments results in more legal trouble. There is one exception, and that is the widow/widower. This could be due to age since more people are widowed when they are older. Crime rates among those who are fifty and older are much lower than in any other age group.

5.3   Family Structure and Interpersonal Violence

This brings the third and final hypothesis into scope: children who grow up in homes without both an adult male and female present are more likely to engage in interpersonal violence than those children who grow up in a traditional nuclear family or one similar to it. Tables 4 and 5 show correlations for male homes which do not have a female present and female headed households, without a male present, with homicide 85, assault 85, and rape 85. Male homes correlate only with rape 85, not with either homicide 85 or assault 85. Female-headed homes show strong correlations with all three forms of interpersonal violence. Regressions showing each of their effects are below in table 8. Warm winters and Southernness are brought in for comparison also.

Table 8

Regression Using Male Homes and Female-headed Households as the Independent Variables and Homicide 85, Assault 85, Rape 85, Warm winters, and Southernness as the Dependent Variables

	Homicide 85	Assault 85	Rape 85	Warm Winter	Southernness
Male Homes Beta	0.15	0.28	0.47	0.00	-.33
R	0.06	0.19	0.38	-.05	-.36
Female Headed Beta	0.59	0.60	0.57	0.33	0.24
R	0.57	0.56	0.50	0.33	0.29
Explained Variance	34%	39%	46%	11%	19%

Significance level 0.01

Analyzing each category, male homes have a non-significant correlation with homicide, a weaker correlation with assault, and a strong correlation with rape. For female-headed households, there are strong relationships for each type of crime. This suggests a possible link to the third hypothesis, since in each of these homes only one adult of either sex is present.

As far as the effect of warm winters or Southernness, there was no relationship between male homes and warm winters and there was an inverse relationship between male homes and Southernness, which perhaps means that most male homes are in either the Midwest, East, or even the West (although parts of the West have warm winters), in the states that do not have warm winters. Female-headed households, on the other hand, show strong and weak relationships to warm winters and Southernness, respectively. A closer look at this topic from an individual standpoint may clarify these results better. The following tables (9 and 10) show families headed by only a female parent and any arrests, and the different types of parenting and any arrests.

Table 9

Cross-tabulation Between any Arrests and Mom Family

Row: any arrests
Column: Mom Family

	Not Mom Family	Mom Family	Total
No	89%	80%	88%
Yes	11%	20%	2%
Total	100%	100%	100%

Table 10

Cross-tabulation Between any Arrests and Parenting

Row: any arrests

Column: Parenting

	Parents	Parent and Stepparent	Mother Only	Relatives	Total
No	89.3%	86.5%	80.4%	88.1%	88.2%
Yes	10.7%	13.5%	19.6%	11.9%	11.8%
Total	100%	100%	100%	100%	100%

The results from the survey data confirm the postulate that more children engage in criminal activity if they live with only one parent, in this case their mother. Examining the data of other types of families, table 10 shows the arrests when living with two parents, a parent and stepparent (both are nuclear family prototypes), only a mother, and with relatives. It is not possible to infer clear data from households that are characterized as headed by relatives because the family setting is not clear enough, in terms of a nuclear family or otherwise.

Still, the evidence points to the fact that more people are arrested when they come from a single parent or guardian home. The types of arrests are not known, but it is safe to say that there is less need for conformity when there are less social attachments as is demonstrated in the single parent/guardian homes.

This is also substantiated by the fact that single mothers now head nearly 50 percent of all homes. Again, this could account for the higher crime rates in the South, because as was noted in the previous section, table 8, more single-mom families exist in the warm winter areas. If one looks at it from the inverse point of view, table 10 shows that children who grow up in a family where both parents are present have the lowest arrest rate. The couples' correlations also support this. The one assumption is that more of these couples have children than not. Where more couples exist, the crime rates are lowest.

Conclusion

The findings suggest that climate and social attachments may have a greater impact on these rates than region. The results do little to satisfy either side of the argument and probably create another side from which to argue. These studies indicate several findings that offer alternative explanations for the higher interpersonal crime rates that plague the South.

First, the South has historically had the largest population of any region in the United States. The migration of citizens from around the country to the South increases the population density, resulting in the emergence of a criminogenic that may result in a greater crime rate.

There are fewer couples and more socially unattached people in the South. More children grow up in homes without two parents than in any other area. There are more strangers and newcomers in the South than ever before. Warm winters have more effect on violent crime rates than being geographically south even though these two variables were initially highly correlated. All of these areas need more exploration in breadth and depth.

Based on the doubt that has been presented in this research and the questions raised by other researchers' work, there appears to be a lack of evidence to substantiate this criminological theory of the Southern subculture of violence.

Appendix A

STATE RATES – Include the following states: Maryland, Washington DC, Virginia, West Virginia, North Carolina, South Carolina, Georgia, Florida, Kentucky, Tennessee, Alabama, Mississippi, Arkansas, Louisiana, Oklahoma, and Texas.

Homicide 85 – homicides per 100,000 in 1985

Assault 85 – assaults per 100,000 in 1985

Rape 85 – rapes per 100,000 in 1985 (Alaska, 77.2, is treated as missing data)

Murder 60 – homicides per 100,000 in 1960

Assault 60 – assaults per 100,000 in 1960

Rape 60 – rapes per 100,000 in 1960

Population Shift – percent population growth (or decline) in 1970-80

Couples – percent of households that contained a married couple in 1980

Male Homes – homes without an adult female per 1,000 in 1980

Female Headed – percent of households headed by a woman with kids 18 and under in 1980

Divorce – annual number of divorces per 1,000 in 1980 (Nevada, 15.4, is omitted)

Median Age – median age of the population in 1980

Southernness – degree of latitude south of the North Pole, based on location of state

Warm Winter – January average low temperature

No move 60 – percent living in same house in 1960 as in 1955

% Poor 79 – percent of families below official poverty line in 1979

% Poor 60 – percent of families below official poverty line in 1960

Appendix B

Any Arrests – have you ever been picked up by the police?
Year – year of survey
Region – residence in 4 major regions
Movers – where did you live at the age of 16? (Region)
Home at 16 – where did you live at the age 16? (Family)
Marital Status – current marital status
Divorce – have you ever been divorced?
Parenting – with whom did you live with at age 16?
Mom Family – were you raised in a female-headed family?
*all data excerpted from Rodney Stark's software package
- Showcase Live, 1989

Bibliography

Ball-Rokeach, Sandra. "Values and Violence: A Test of the Subculture of Violence Thesis." American Sociological Review 38 (December 1973): 736—749.

Baron, Larry and Straus, Murray. "Cultural and Economic Sources of Homicide in the United States." The Sociological Quarterly 29 (1988): 371—390.

Brearly, H.C. "The Patterns of Violence." Culture in the South. Edited by W. T. Couch 1934:678—692. Chapel Hill: University of North Carolina Press.

Bursik Jr., Robert J. "Social Delinquency: Problems and Prospects." Criminology 26 (1988): 519—551.

Cohen, Lawrence E. and Jim Webb. "Community Change and Patterns of Delinquency." American Journal of Delinquency 18 (1982):138—164.

Davis, James A. and Tom W. Smith. General Social Surveys, 1972—1987. Principal Investigator, James A. Davis; Senior Study Director, Tom W. Smith. NORC ed. Chicago: National Opinion Research Center, producer, 1987; Storrs, CT: The Roper Center for Public Opinion Research, University of Connecticut, Distributor.

Dixon, Jo and Lizotte, Alan. "Gun Ownership and the 'Southern Subculture of Violence'." American Journal of Sociology 93 (September 1987): 383—405.

Doerner, William G. "A Regional Analysis of Homicide Rates in the United States." Criminology 13 (1) (1975): 90—101.

Doerner, William G. "The Index of Southernness Revisited." Criminology 16 (1) (1978): 47—67.

Erlanger, Howard S. "Is There a Subculture of Violence in the South?" Journal of Criminal Law and Criminology 66 (4) (1976): 483—490.

Flanagan, Timothy and Kathleen Maguire, eds. Sourcebook of Criminal Justice Statistics – 1989. U.S. Department of Justice, Bureau of Justice Statistics. Washington, DC: USGPO (1990).

Gastil, Raymond. "Homicide and a Regional Culture of Violence." American Sociological Review 36 (1971): 412—427.

Hackney, Sheldon. "Southern Violence." American Historical Review 74 (1974): 906—925.

Hartnagel, Timothy. "Subculture of Violence: Further Evidence." Pacific Sociological Review 23 (2) (1980): 217—242.

Hawley, F. Frederick and Steven F. Messner. "The Southern Violence Construct: A Review of the Arguments, Evidence, and the Normative Context." Justice Quarterly 6 (4) 1989: 481—511.

Hepburn, John R. "Violent Behavior in Interpersonal Relationships." The Sociological Quarterly 14 (1973): 419—429.

Huff-Corzine, Lin; Corzine, Jay; and Moore, David. "Southern Exposure: Deciphering the South's Influence on Homicide Rates." Social Forces 64 (June 1986): 906—924.

Lester, David "A Regional Analysis of Suicide and Homicide Rates in the USA: Search for Broad Cultural Patterns." <u>Social Psychiatry and Epidemiology</u> 23 (1988): 202—205.

Loftin, Colin and Hill, Robert. "Regional Subculture and Homicide: An Examination of the Gastil-Hackney Thesis." <u>American Sociological Review</u> 39 (October 1974): 714—724.

Luckenbill, David F. and Daniel P. Doyle. "Structural Position and Violence: Developing a Cultural Explanation." <u>Criminology</u> 27 (3) (1989): 419—436.

McCarty, John D., Omer R. Galle, and W. Zimmern. "Population Density, Social Structure, and Interpersonal Violence: An Intermetropolitan Test of Competing Models." <u>American Behavioral Scientist</u> 18 (1975): 771—91.

Messener, Steven F. "Regional and Racial Effects on the Urban Homicide Rates." American Journal of Sociology 88 (1983): 997—1007.

Messener, Steven F. "Regional Differences in the Economic Correlates of the Urban Homicide Rates: Some Evidence on the Importance of a Cultural Context." <u>Criminology</u> 24 (4) (1983): 477—488.

Parker, Robert Nash. "Poverty, Subculture of Violence, and Type of Homicide." <u>Social Forces</u> 67 (4) (1989): 983—1007.

Poland, James M. "Structural of Violence: Youth Offender Value Systems." <u>Criminal Justice and Behavior</u> 5(2) (1978): 159—164.

Singleton, Royce; Straits, Bruce; Straits, Margaret; and McAllister, Ronald. <u>Approaches to Social Research</u>. New York: Oxford University Press, 1988.

Stark, Rodney. "Introducing Criminology through the Computer." <u>Computer Handbook</u>. Showcase Presentational Software. W. Lafayette, IN, 1989.

Wolfgang, Marvin. <u>Patterns in Criminal Homicide</u>. Philadelphia: University of Pennsylvania Press, (1958).

Wolfgang, Marvin and Franco Ferracuti. <u>The Southern Subculture of Violence</u>. London: Tavistock Publications.

Coming Soon:

Soukaina Preview

Twenty-six-year-old Soukaina, a native of Morocco, has never left her country. Employed at a school, she seeks a worthy man with whom to spend the rest of her life. Married for eleven years and the father of three, Adam has lived a life of contradictions. Residing worlds apart, Soukaina and Adam find solace from each other through their letters.

With his wife and children away in his wife's home country, Adam combats his loneliness by corresponding with Soukaina. As they write letters back and forth, they discover they are soul mates and vow to share their dreams, their hopes, and their lives. But will their love survive the distance and the challenges of their complicated lives?

Cup of Coffee Preview

I know that I have the experience to live on the ground level, forced to live a happy life.

I have to sacrifice for my family, but I find such contentious relationships have messed me up.

Close your eyes and all the pain will go away and you will find peace within yourself.

I am here to value you and to make every moment a special one that could be an amazing one.

I crave such relation without the traditional boundaries that ail marriages every day.

I shall confess that I have broken the tradition and let my feeling become my law in this course of life.

He stayed awake and decided to walk with me on the beach. The cool air of the morning mist hit his face. It felt incredibly peaceful. He had forgotten what love felt like—this love took him absolutely by surprise. It gave him such an amazing feeling that he was preparing to go on a journey of providence. He was absolutely amazed by the sound of the waves. It made him feel rejuvenated and he reached the platonic climax. The amazing feeling gave him such energy. A journey is an endurance challenge, but more accurately, it is fate!

The Immortal Tree Preview

He continued to hold her hand; her touch gave comfort and strength to him. Words were spoken: marry me without paper—he felt relief. They exchanged kisses on the road while walking—each one helping the other to forget the struggles they had faced.

She told him that he should continue on his journey and that twenty-eight months would pass so quickly. They looked at each other quizzically. Near his home, hands were about to separate. He gave her one last squeeze. Confidently she smiled and took another kiss. After a few more kisses, he looked back to see their whereabouts.

It was a beautiful moment, but they did not stop kissing. They continued to travel joyful journeys together. As she was kissing him, his heart was suddenly blinded by an intense light. It shone so brightly that the whole world was illuminated. Small, innocent birth sleeping.

As they reached his home, he realized that he just had to make the decision to be with her. You feel more urgent as you look back along the journey—it seemed so long without her. He started to grow weary of walking, hoping that someday soon he will rest a while with her. The feeling grew, but he stubbornly fought it.

He relaxed and closed his eyes. Ah, this is what it feels like to love and be loved. He continued to sleep, dreaming of the day he will awaken between her arms.

About the Author:

Hassan Dibich, a United States citizen, was born in Casablanca, Morocco. He studied theology in Leuven, Belgium, and law in Strasbourg, France. He currently is a professor of French and Spanish at Richard Bland College, College of William and Mary.